Passion, Possession and Obsession.

Emily-Maria Pearce

Passion, Possession and Obsession. © 2022
Emily-Maria Pearce

All rights reserved.

No part of this publication may be reproduced, stored in a retrieval system, or transmitted, in any form or by any means, electronic, mechanical, photocopying, recording or otherwise, without the prior written permission of the presenters.

Emily-Maria Pearce asserts the moral right to be identified as author of this work.

Presentation by *BookLeaf Publishing*

Web: www.bookleafpub.com

E-mail: info@bookleafpub.com

ISBN: 978-93-95755-96-2

First edition 2022

DEDICATION

To you, A.

I promise to try to be less insane.

I can't promise that I won't be somewhat obsessed for you forever. If I am honest I'll probably always be the president of the AM fan club. I mean it's been 25 years so you might as well have me forever.

ACKNOWLEDGEMENT

To the 2 people who have helped me through this;
Tracy, thank you for trying to make me see sense.
Emily, thank you for helping me with 'the right thing to do'.

PREFACE

I am crazy.

Joking aside, crazy is really a word we shouldn't use. It infers that only certain types of thoughts and behaviours are 'normal'. That said, I feel like if anyone else witnessed these thoughts they would describe me as crazy. Anyone else in my situation would be happy right? They wouldn't experience intrusive and distracting thoughts?

Poetry has allowed me to notice, experience and journal these entirely valid feelings.

My Muse

I love:

Sunrises and sunsets.
Living life to the fullest, no regrets.
The moon and shooting stars,
driving fast in expensive cars.

The taste of real Champagne
and memories of walks along the Seine.

Morning walks and kinky sex,
and playing vintage mixed cassettes.

But my biggest muse of all is also potentially my
biggest downfall.

The Girl with the Golden Hair.

Love or Limerence?

Limerence

An all consuming passion,
intrusive thoughts that are distracting.
A state of romantic infatuation,
I live for moments of us interacting.

Love is described as deep affection,
attraction and sexual desire.
Devotion, protection and connection,
All I know is I want to set you on fire.

So am I suffering limerence?
I do have obsessive personality traits.
It feels like love so what's the difference?
To childhood does this all date?

Are you replacing something missing?
Or is this something in my brain?
Causing me to imagine it's you I'm kissing
It's like you're my cocaine.

The Girl with the Golden Hair

& when I think about that night, the most important night of my life.

I think about you, looking in the mirror, brushing your lush golden hair. Unaware of your breath taking beauty.

I replay that over and over. In hindsight, that moment was when I realised that I am in love with you.

Voyage

Rewinding back to the Voyage we took in May,
there was such a lot going on that day,
so I didn't say all I wanted to say.

I got so caught up in the emotion of the event,
I didn't tell you what you represent
or that I believe you're an angel that heaven sent.

I wish I walked you to the station,
one more chance for uninterrupted conversation,
but I'm grateful you accepted the invitation.

I never thought you'd know my name,
but your friendship was my aim
because I know you'll never feel the same.

Obsessed with Obsession

I am obsessed with obsession,
Intrusive thoughts surrounding you,
that is my confession.

I need you in my possession,
You are the most beautiful woman to grace this earth,
I am obsessed with obsession.

Is this a childhood regression?
I think I am addicted to you.
That is my confession.

I must make a good impression,
constant self improvement will make me more
attractive?
I am obsessed with obsession.

Poetry is my self-expression,
I wish I could share these thoughts with you.
That is my confession.

Does all this matter? That is the question.
Deep down I know you'll never be mine.
I am obsessed with obsession.
That is my confession.

55.8483° N, 4.4933° W

When things get tough and I just can't cope,
It's you I see, you give me hope.

In my mind I see your sultry smile
and it makes me happy for a little while.

Every word you sing, each flawless note,
I let it engulf me and away I float.

Into a fantasy, a passionate illusion,
a place where I have no confusion.

Curled up by the fire, the house smells of pine,
every second with you is so divine.

Walks along the beach at night.
Talking until the morning light.

Holding hands, kissing like teens
because after all, you are my queen.

In this place I am finally me.
Responsibilities gone, I am free.

The White Hart Inn

We meet for a drink at the White Hart Inn,
it feels so risky in your home town.
You order us a local gin,
and ask me to sit down.

I feel like I've known you forever,
you make me feel like I am home.
I love hearing your stories, you are so clever,
about our favourite palindrome.

I feel I'm seeing glimpses of the real you,
talking about your son.
This fantasy I must pursue,
because I feel like you're the only one.

You show me more affection,
with each and every drink.
Each story strengthens our connection,
could I be your missing link?

I am addicted to your energy,
I get high from looking in your eyes.
Every moment we share engrained in my
memory,
as you place your hand on my thighs.

I've always needed to feel this close,
to be the one you trust.
I want to be the one you love the most,
this is not just lust.

When I Dream I'm Alone with You

Your passion takes me by surprise as you push me
into the room.
Pinned against the wall you trace my lips with your
fingertips.
I comb back your hair, inhaling your perfume.
You kiss me, I savour the feeling of your lips on
mine.
Our fingers are interlocked as your tongue enters my
mouth.
Your kiss tells me you want me.
My hand travels up your thighs and I start to unbutton
your jeans.
You unzip the back of my dress, kissing my neck.
You lead me to the bed.

In your arms I find the solace I desperately crave.
This is what my body was made for.
My tongue writes our future on your body.
Your heart beat is intoxicating.
Your laboured breathing tells me you feel the same.
I love seeing your feet curl with pleasure, I am drunk
from tasting you.

Rhythm of the Rain

I lie in bed listening to the rain,
I can't help but hear it echoing your name.

Like a siren, calling, pulling me in
and once again I'm drowning in your milky skin.

Your legs wrapped around me, our lips locked
tight.
The rain isn't the wettest thing tonight.

Come Play my Secret Game

Underneath your coat you're wearing your work
uniform;
blue eyeshadow, silk dress and white platforms.
Your gaze alone gives me a shiver
I'm dying to be the reason you quiver.

You guide my hand onto your thigh,
you can't help but let out a little sigh.
I desperately pull your lace to the side
so I can slide my fingers right inside.

You begin to drip down my wrist,
give in to the pleasure don't resist.
I begin to feel your body shake,
your moans make my heart ache....

Control

As I close my eyes I see your hand pulling me
towards you...

You're standing by the window pane,
the room lit by candlelight.
You're softly singing and you call out my name,
seducing me into the night of my life.

In a satin gown and black lace lingerie,
Your confidence gives me goosebumps as you
beg me to play,

You lick me, kiss me, taste me, suck me and
taste me,
love bites ensure that I am yours.
I feel like I am in ecstasy,
onto your lips I pour.

I surrender myself so easily to your kiss,
it feels like we've done this before.
On this moment I will reminisce,
I promise to love you forever more.

My Love, My Life

Sometimes I wonder how I got in so deep,
I appeared to fall so fast.
I'm counting down the time until I can sleep,
so once again you'll be in my grasp.

A walk in the woods, a wine by the fire,
but your company is not all I desire.....

With your tongue you gently caress my lips
and I can't help pushing against your hips.
My hand running up your inner thigh
because a kiss like that does not lie.

My Sagittarius

I used to wonder what I would actually say to you if I had the chance.

Now I realise, I would say nothing.

I'd only need to kiss you, that kiss would speak a thousand words.

The Moon

If I am honest, I struggle with quotes such as:

"No matter where you are, you will always be
looking at the same moon I am".

The reality for us is:

As you're looking at the moon,
for me the sun is rising.
I wish our souls to be attuned,
there is no compromising.

Geographically you are 16,807 km away
and between us there is 22 years.
2 men, 3 kids standing in our way
When will these feelings disappear?

Essence of You

A strand of your hair.
The twinkle of your eyes.
The glimmer of your smile.
Your softly spoken Scottish lilt.

The essence of you. That is what runs through
my veins.

When You Really Loved Someone

& the saddest part isn't that you don't love me.
It's that my love is wasted because you'll never
know how I feel.

& the most heart breaking part isn't that you're
not my soul mate.
It's that I will spend the rest of my life wishing
that you were.

IX.XII.MCMLXVII

I am scared.

I am scared that one day, your face won't be the first thing I see in my mind when I awake.

Thoughts of you carry me when I cannot carry myself.

I am scared to let you go.

This Side Wins

19

I hope he wakes you up by kissing your back,
with a perfectly brewed cup of tea.
I hope that your relationship is without a crack,
because you mean the world to me.

I hope he constantly reminds you that you're so
beautiful
and realises he is the world's luckiest man.
I hope his love is indisputable
and has been since you began.

I hope that you are both connected
and that he is your best friend.
Most importantly I hope you feel protected,
with him, I'll never contend.

Let Go

It takes a lot of courage to let go of something you love.

Letting go doesn't mean I love you any less, it means that I need to start loving myself.

When the sun rises, I think of you, when darkness falls, I am thinking of you.
Thoughts of you mean that I am missing the potential beauty in so much of what's around me, things that could really make me happy.

You've already found your happily ever after and now it's my turn to try and save what I have.

There is a difference between goodbye and letting go. A, I let you go because you were never mine.

Tomorrow I will need to let you go again and then again the next day. Until one day, you will be gone because, it's getting too heavy to hold on.

Perfume In The Breeze

21

Everytime I hear your voice in the wind,
everytime I smell your perfume in the breeze,
everytime my heartaches for you,
I am grateful, you have given me poetry.

This isn't where it ends

This isn't where it ends.

We search for a connection between heart, soul, body and mind.

Our body seeks affection and excitement.
Our intuitive mind craves someone who can nourish our desire to learn.
Our soul searches for someone who allows us to forget our inhibitions and insecurities and understands our emotions.
Our heart seeks love and intimacy.

This isn't where it ends.

Affection.Intimacy.Love.Emotion.Excitement.N ourishment.

This isn't where it ends.

www.ingramcontent.com/pod-product-compliance
Lightning Source LLC
LaVergne TN
LVHW021351200726

843509LV00014B/2795

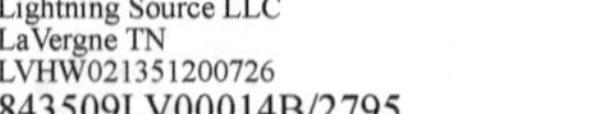